My CHRISTMAS Planner

Name

WWW.LITTLEPOPOFCOLOUR.COM

ALL ABOUT ME

How old am I?

What am I like?

My favourite colour

My favourite food

My favourite things

Where am I for Christmas this year?

My Family

My Pets

This Year So Far

Top Achievements

Best Books

Proud of

Challenges

My Birthday

Kind things

Moments I'll Always Remember

Health

New Friends

Low Points

Music

Top TV

Favourite Movies

HOPES AND DREAMS

What I want to learn

What I want to make

Where I want to go

What I want to achieve

What I want to feel

Who I want to be

My Christmas Wishlist

GIFT IDEAS

For   **Ideas**

For	Ideas

MORE GIFT IDEAS

For   *Ideas*

For　　　　　Ideas

1	2	3	4
8	9	10	11
15	16	17	18
22	23	24 Christmas Eve	25 Christmas
29	30	31 New Year's Eve	

Let's get planning

Food Ideas

RECIPES

MORE RECIPES

Shopping List

NOTES and IDEAS

CHRISTMAS CARDS

For	Address or Email	Sent

For	Address or Email	Sent

There's more planning

Christmas tree

Stockings

Tree decorations

Decorations for indoors

Outdoor decorations

to be done, you know!

Table setting and decor

Shopping List

Get TV Ready

What's on?	Day	Time	Channel

NOTES and REMINDERS

Christmas Games

Christmas Activities

CHRISTMAS DAY
schedule

BOXING DAY schedule

Extra Lists

Extra Lists

Still to do...

ULTIMATE CHECKLIST

- ☐ Food ordered
- ☐ Drink ordered
- ☐ Tinsel
- ☐ Menu planned
- ☐ Buy gifts
- ☐ Stocking fillers
- ☐ Secret Santa
- ☐ Wrapping paper
- ☐ Buy Christmas cards
- ☐ Gifts wrapped
- ☐ Christmas cards sent
- ☐ Tree
- ☐ Mat for beneath the tree
- ☐ Tree decorations
- ☐ Baubles
- ☐ Tinsel
- ☐ Fairy lights
- ☐ Stockings
- ☐ Other indoor decorations
- ☐ Wreath
- ☐ Outdoor lights
- ☐ Other outdoor decorations
- ☐ Extension cable
- ☐ Tablecloth
- ☐ Napkins
- ☐ Placecards
- ☐ Party favours
- ☐ Flowers/centrepiece
- ☐ Christmas crackers
- ☐ Snacks
- ☐ Plan activities
- ☐ Buy TV Guide
- ☐ Plan what to watch
- ☐ Record movies in advance
- ☐ Snacks for Santa
- ☐ Christmas playlist
- ☐ Food cooked/prepped
- ☐ Drinks in the fridge
- ☐ Table set
- ☐ Phone charged
- ☐ Phone storage OK
- ☐ Tidy house

X-MAS

CHRISTMAS EVE

Where?

With whom?

Last minute prep

What I did

Best part of the day

Photos

CHRISTMAS

Oh the weather outside was...

Who was there

Best thing we did

Worst thing we did

DAY!

Best gift received

Most memorable moment

What made me smile?

What we watched

Best food I ate

Photos

Funny things

MY GIFTS

From	Gift received

BOXING DAY

Shopping

Eating

TV

Napping

Best part of the day

Photos

NOTES
for next year

Gifts

Food

What we have

...and where it is

What we need

What worked

What didn't work

Remember...

27th December

Photos

Friends

Memories

Ideas

28th December

Outings

Doodles

Photos

Shopping

29th December

Photos

Friends

Memories

Ideas

30th December

Outings

Doodles

Photos

Shopping

NEW YEAR'S EVE
plans

Plans

Ideas

NEW YEAR'S DAY plans

Plans

Ideas

NEW YEAR'S

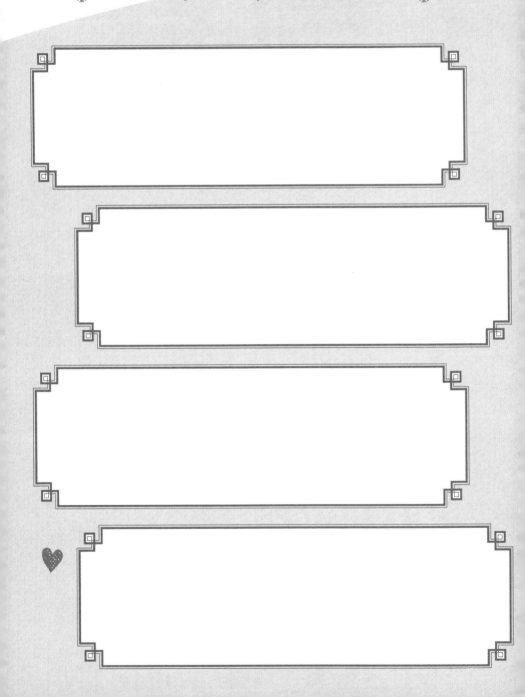

RESOLUTIONS

© SHARI BLACK 2020
ISBN: 9798661242730

WWW.LITTLEPOPOFCOLOUR.COM

Made in the USA
Monee, IL
22 September 2020